*All About Your*

# Brain

Donna Bailey

STECK-VAUGHN
LIBRARY
A Division of Steck-Vaughn Company
*Austin, Texas*

# How to Use This Book

This book tells you many things about your brain and nervous system. There is a Table of Contents on the next page. It shows you what each double page of the book is about. For example, pages 10 and 11 tell you about "The Nervous System."

On most of these pages you will find some words that are printed in **bold** type. The bold type shows you that these words are in the Glossary on pages 46 and 47. The Glossary explains the meaning of some words that may be new to you.

At the very end of the book there is an Index. The Index tells you where to find certain words in the book. For example, you can use it to look up words like axon, spinal cord, cerebrum, neurons, and many other words to do with your brain and nervous system.

**Library of Congress Cataloging-In-Publication Data**

Bailey, Donna.
  All about your brain / Donna Bailey.
    p.  cm. — (Health facts)
  Includes index.
  Summary: Discusses the enormous capabilities of our sophisticated brain.
    ISBN 0-8114-2778-1
    1. Brain—Juvenile literature. 2. Neurophysiology—Juvenile literature. [1. Brain.] I. Title. II. Series: Bailey, Donna.
  Health facts.
  QP976.B252   1990
  612.8'2—dc20                                    90-41008
                                                    CIP AC

# Contents

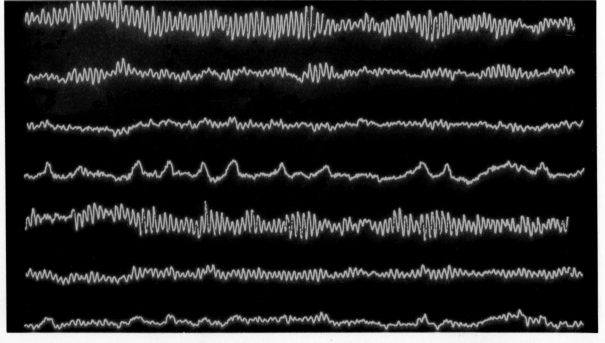

## Introduction

Your **brain** controls what you do, think, or feel.

**Nerves** carry messages to and from the brain along your **nervous system.** The part of the brain where you remember and think is called the mind.

**this chimp is using a twig as a tool to help dig up ants**

Some animals, like sheep, have very little **intelligence** and are unable to use their brains very much. Sheepdogs are more intelligent. They can work out how to make sheep go into a pen. Chimpanzees are very clever animals. Like humans, they can learn to use tools to do different jobs.

People have the best brains of all. We use our brains to work out very complicated things, like how to play a computer game.

# Long Ago

A long time ago people knew that the head was an important part of the body but they did not know anything about the brain. Chiefs and rulers wore headdresses or crowns to show they were the "head" of their people.

Over 2,000 years ago Greek doctors knew that the brain helps us think. They knew the brain also helps us to see, hear, smell, taste, and feel through our five **senses.**

The Romans knew that the brain is used for learning, but not how it worked. Even 600 years ago, doctors did not know how to treat the brain.

People thought that the **heart** was at the center of everything we felt and did.

**Roman children studying**

**doctors with a patient**

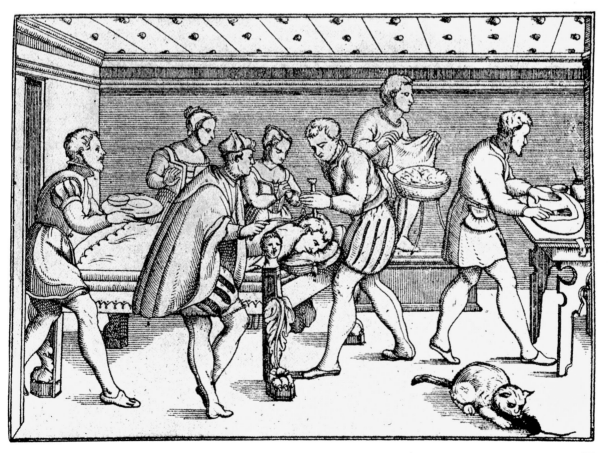

7

# Finding Out

About 400 years ago a Belgian named Vesalius said that thoughts and feelings came from the brain, not the heart. Then William Harvey showed that the heart is a pump to push **blood** around the body.

**Luigi Galvani**

**people with illnesses of the brain were locked up in chains like criminals**

Later Galvani discovered that electricity made the legs of dead frogs twitch.

8

Doctors then began to realize that different parts of the brain control different parts of the body.

Many people thought that a person's character could be told by feeling bumps on the head.

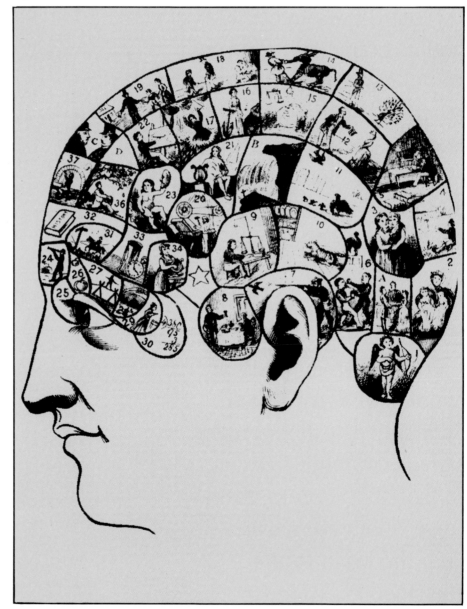

this old map of the head shows which parts were thought to control our feelings and talents

# The Nervous System

Your brain and your **spinal cord** make up the **central nervous system.**

Most nerves in our bodies branch out from the spinal cord to divide and reach every part of the body. This outer network of nerves is called the **peripheral nervous system.** The spinal cord carries signals to and from the peripheral nervous system and the brain.

Each nerve is made of bundles of nerve **fibers. Sensory** nerve fibers carry signals from the five senses to the brain. **Motor** nerve fibers carry signals from the brain to the **muscles.**

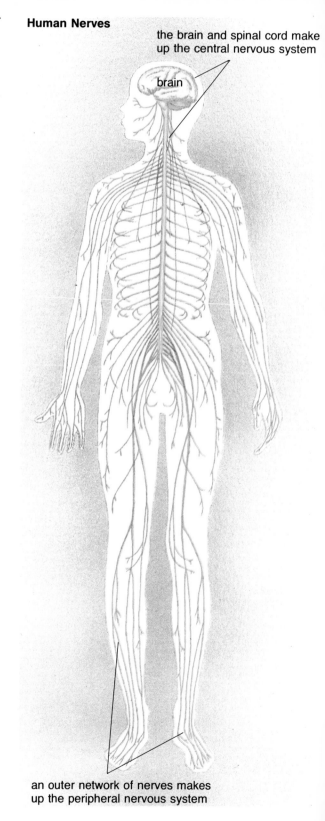

the brain and spinal cord make up the central nervous system

brain

an outer network of nerves makes up the peripheral nervous system

10

**nerves carry messages like the wires of a telephone system**

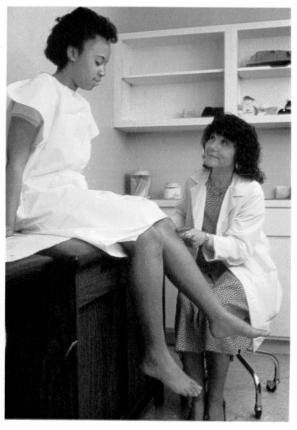

Some nerves work without you thinking what to do. If you touch something hot, the pain signal travels quickly along the sensory nerve fibers to the spinal cord. At the same time another signal goes straight from the spinal cord to the muscles, so you pull your arm away by **reflex** action.

**testing a reflex action**

11

# How Nerves Work

Each nerve in the peripheral nervous system is made up of a bundle of nerve **cells** called **neurons** which pick up signals from the muscles or skin. The signals travel from one neuron to another in short bursts, or pulses, of electricity.

**A Neuron**

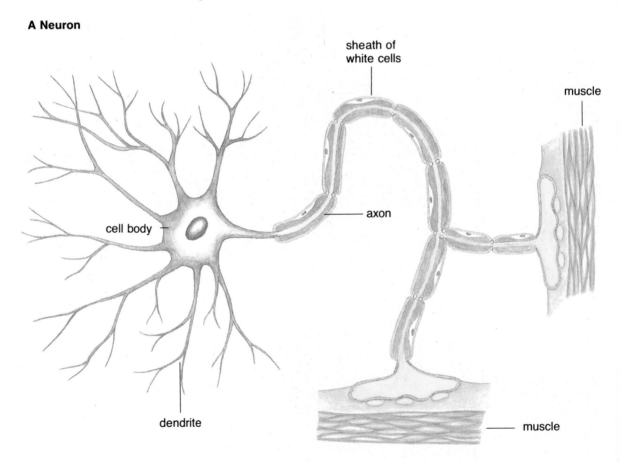

sheath of white cells

muscle

axon

cell body

dendrite

muscle

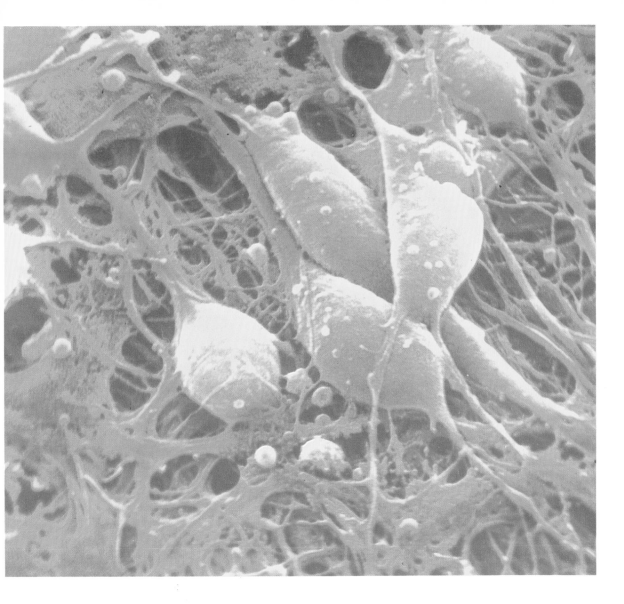

The photograph of neurons was taken under a **microscope.**

Each neuron has a cell body with a long tail called the **axon.** Hair-like fibers called **dendrites** pick up pulses from the nearby neurons and pass the message along the chain.

# The Brain

Between the cells of the brain and the bones of the skull are three thin **membranes** called the **meninges.**
  Inside the brain, the **cerebrum,** which controls all **voluntary** movements, thought, and memory is covered by a wrinkled layer of **cortex.** The **pons** links the back of the brain to the middle section.

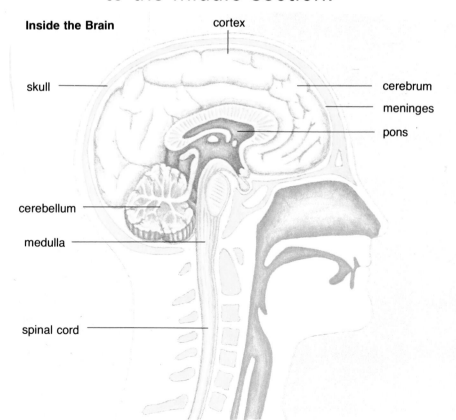

**Inside the Brain**

cortex

skull

cerebrum

meninges

pons

cerebellum

medulla

spinal cord

**the brain is protected by the bones of the skull**

**the brain is much more complicated than the inside of a computer**

The **cerebellum** makes sure all parts of the body work together and helps you keep your balance. The **medulla** looks after your heart, breathing, and **digestion.**

# The Spinal Cord

The brain and the spinal cord are made of **gray matter** and **white matter.** Gray matter, found in the center of the spinal cord, is made up of the cell bodies of motor neurons. Gray matter is surrounded by a layer of white matter made up of nerve fibers. The spinal cord runs from the brain down the hollow centers of the bones, or vertebrae, of the spine.

A few nerves in the head are the only ones that go straight to the brain. The rest of the nerves pass through the spinal cord first. Each nerve contains both sensory and motor neurons.

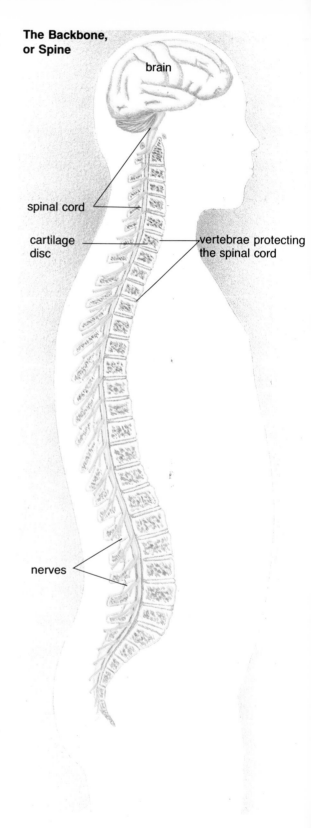

The Backbone, or Spine

brain

spinal cord

cartilage disc

vertebrae protecting the spinal cord

nerves

16

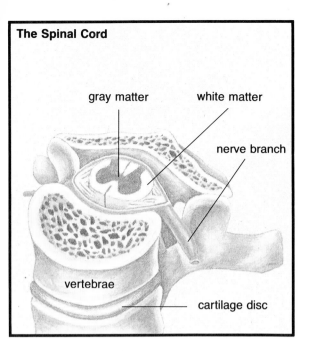

gray matter

white matter

nerve branch

vertebrae

cartilage disc

**we use the support of the spine to carry weights**

**the vertebrae protect the spinal cord**

The top 24 vertebrae of the spine have a **cartilage disc** between them to separate the bones. The discs help cushion the spine from any shocks.

The three thin meninges that cover the brain protect the brain and spinal cord from shocks.

# The Control Center

**Control Area of the Brain**

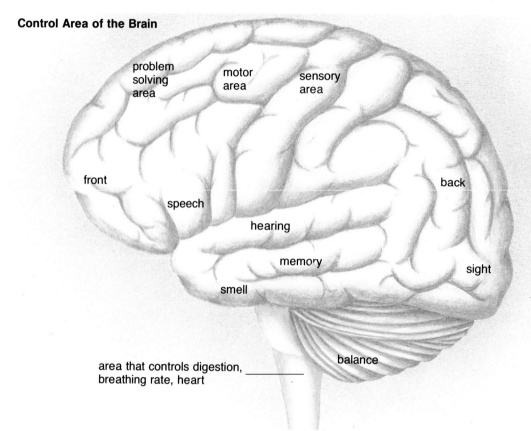

problem solving area

motor area

sensory area

front

back

speech

hearing

memory

sight

smell

balance

area that controls digestion, breathing rate, heart _____

We think and solve problems with the front part of our brain. Farther back, the motor area on each side of the brain controls our muscles. Behind that, the sensory area controls our sense of touch. Other areas of the cerebrum help us see, hear, speak, and remember.

If you want to open a jar of jelly or hit a baseball, the brain receives and sends many different signals. The brain sends messages along the nerves to tell the muscles what to do.

**to open this bottle, the girl uses signals from her sight, smell, taste, and touch**

**a baseball player has to decide the speed and angle of the ball and how to move**

# The Brain and the Senses

The skin has special nerve endings called receptors that record heat, pain, pressure, and touch.

Waves of sound enter the ear and hit the **eardrum.** Three small bones pass the sound to a liquid in a spiral tube. Tiny hairs then change the sound into nerve signals.

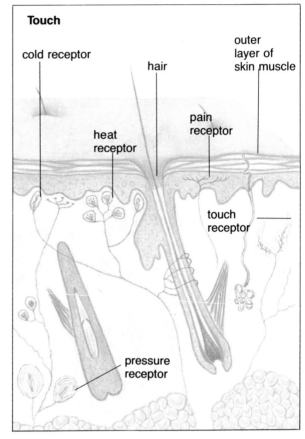

Touch

cold receptor

heat receptor

hair

pain receptor

outer layer of skin muscle

touch receptor

pressure receptor

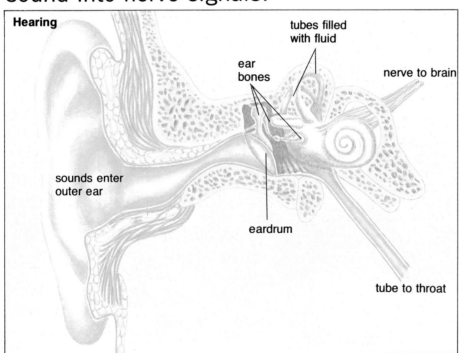

Hearing

tubes filled with fluid

ear bones

nerve to brain

sounds enter outer ear

eardrum

tube to throat

there are nerve endings just below the skin's surface

signals of sound pass up the nerve to the brain

## our five senses tell us about the world around us

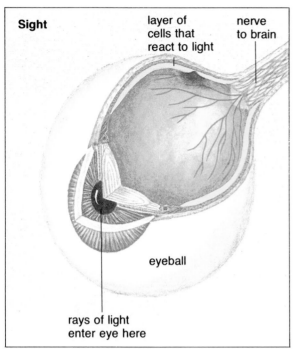

Sight

layer of cells that react to light

nerve to brain

eyeball

rays of light enter eye here

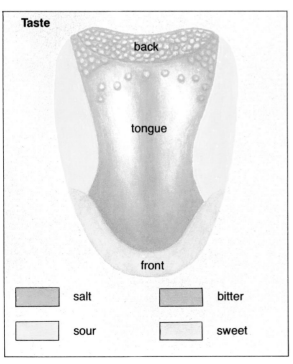

Taste

back

tongue

front

| | |
|---|---|
| salt | bitter |
| sour | sweet |

When you look at something, rays of light go into the eye and hit a layer of cells at the back of the eyeball. Each cell reacts to the light and sends a signal to the brain along the **optic nerve.**

You taste things by getting signals from a group of cells called taste buds on your tongue. The back of the tongue lets you taste bitter things, and you taste sour things along the sides. You taste salty things in the center, and sweet things at the front of the tongue.

Your sense of taste is linked to your sense of smell, which you get from sense cells in your nose. The smell of an onion gives you its taste.

21

# The Brain and Movement

Our bodies move by using muscles. When we want to make a movement, the motor neurons inside a muscle tell it to shorten and bunch up. To move in the opposite direction, a different muscle shortens and the first muscle relaxes.

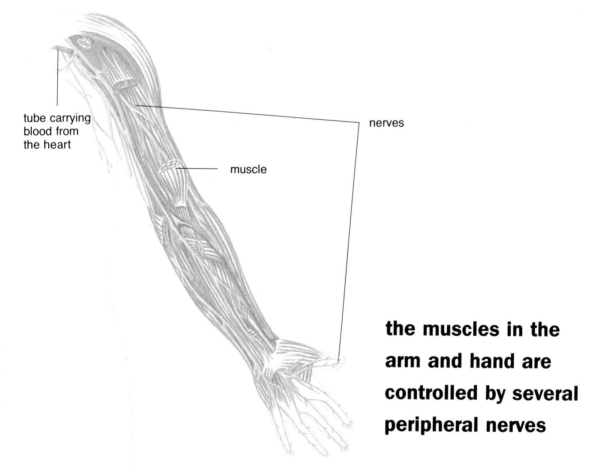

tube carrying blood from the heart

nerves

muscle

**the muscles in the arm and hand are controlled by several peripheral nerves**

## the central nervous system controls our movements

Muscles work in pairs. They cannot get longer but can only shorten and relax.

When you want to bend your leg, your brain sends a signal to the **hamstring** muscle to shorten it. To straighten your leg again, your brain sends a signal to the **quadriceps** muscle.

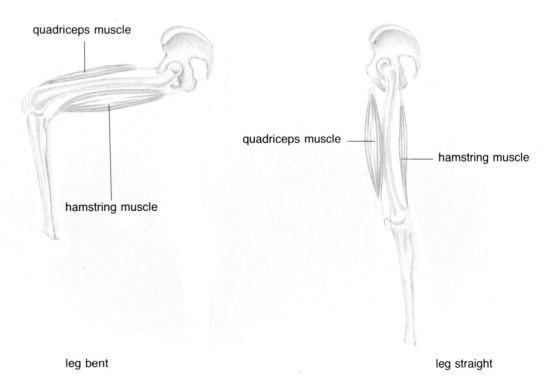

quadriceps muscle

hamstring muscle

quadriceps muscle

hamstring muscle

leg bent

leg straight

23

# Body Control

You send messages around your body either as nerve pulses along neurons, or as special **chemicals** in the blood called **hormones.** Hormones are made in **endocrine glands** and are controlled by the brain.

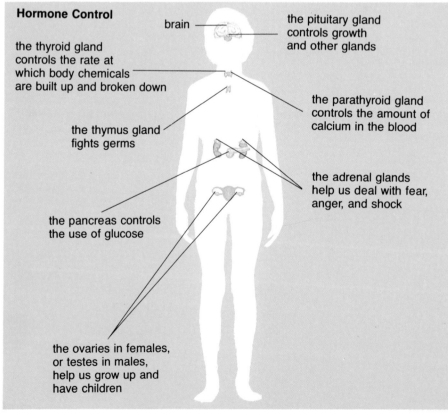

**Hormone Control**

brain

the pituitary gland controls growth and other glands

the thyroid gland controls the rate at which body chemicals are built up and broken down

the parathyroid gland controls the amount of calcium in the blood

the thymus gland fights germs

the adrenal glands help us deal with fear, anger, and shock

the pancreas controls the use of glucose

the ovaries in females, or testes in males, help us grow up and have children

**hormones in endocrine glands control the way your body works**

24

The part of the brain that senses when you get cold from playing in the snow also controls the working of the **pituitary gland** underneath the brain. The pituitary gland controls growth as well as controlling other glands.

If you are excited or afraid, the **adrenal glands** make your heart beat faster and your body gets ready for fast action.

adrenalin pumped into the blood will make you ready to run from a snake

25

# Intelligence and Learning

Both people and animals act by **instinct,** but people are more intelligent than animals. This baby is learning to recognize color, shape, and size.

Our brain can hold a huge amount of information and use it to solve very difficult problems and think out how things work.

**we mainly use the left side of the brain to play chess**

26

Your cerebrum is divided into two halves, which each seem to do different kinds of thinking. You use the left half of the cerebrum for speaking, and solving problems. The right half controls the way you feel and your imagination.

a jazz player uses the right side of the brain to feel the mood of the music

# Memory and Dreams

Memory is the store of things you have seen and done. Some people remember things better than others.

Put some objects on a tray, and you and a friend look at them for a minute. Now try to write down as many of the objects as you can remember. Which of you has the best memory?

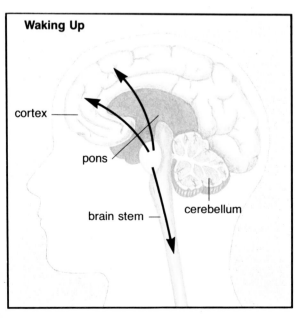

**Waking Up**

cortex

pons

brain stem

cerebellum

Scientists do not really know why we dream. They think the brain may be sorting out the information it stores.

Your brain helps you to wake up from sleeping. Nerve signals from the pons go out to all parts of the brain.

# Brain Power

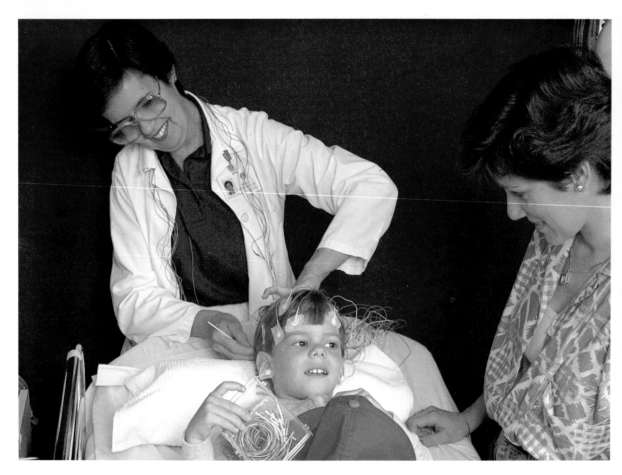

The picture shows a patient with
**electrodes** being put on his head.
These pick up the electrical activity
on the surface of the brain and record
his **brain waves** on a screen. The
machine that does this is called an
EEG machine for short.

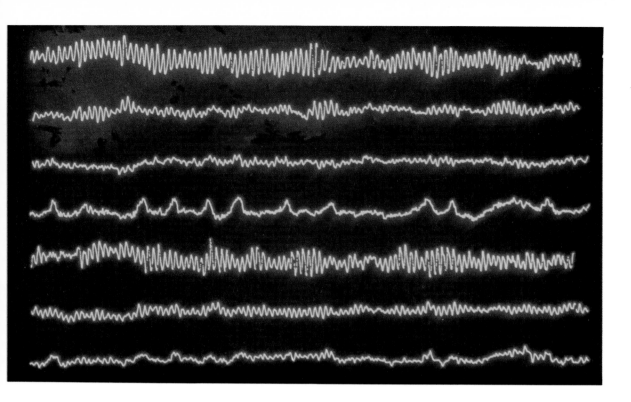

**an EEG read-out**

The EEG read-out in the picture was taken while the patient was asleep. It shows a healthy pattern and no sign of any illness of the nervous system.

Our brain uses electricity to control the whole body. The amount of electricity the body uses would be enough to provide the power for the light in this refrigerator!

# Lifeline

A newborn baby has nearly all its brain cells, but an EEG shows it has hardly any brain waves at all. The cells are quite small and there are few connections between them. As the baby grows and learns how to walk, talk, and get what it needs, the connections form and the brain stores that knowledge.

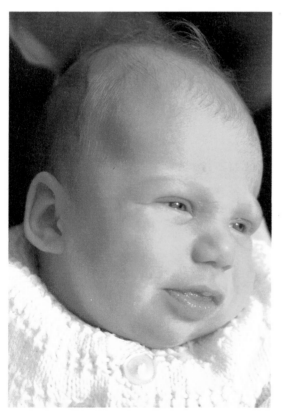

A teenager's brain is fully grown, but new connections between the cells are still being made so new information can be easily learned.

After you are about 25, some of the nerve cells in your brain start to die. An old person's brain has lost many of its brain cells, and few new connections are made.

after an accident, machines can help keep the body working and so give the brain a rest

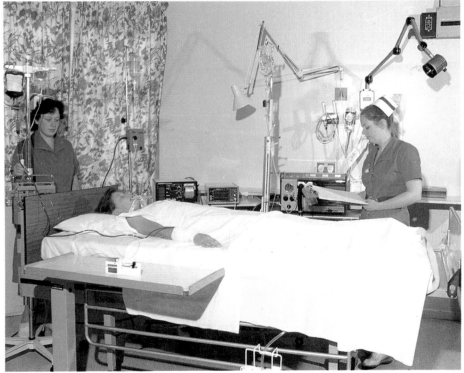

# Illnesses of the Brain

Sometimes things can go wrong with the brain.

The photograph, taken under a microscope, shows a **virus** that attacks the meninges, causing a disease called meningitis.

Changes in the blood supply to the brain can cause severe headaches known as migraines.

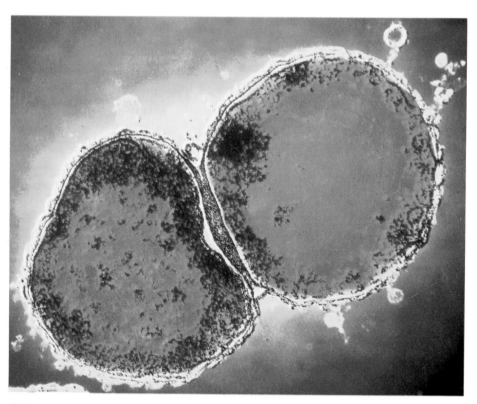

**a craft may help train the brain to learn lost skills**

Abnormal electrical activity in the brain can cause **epilepsy.**

Cutting off the blood supply to the brain causes a **stroke.** The brain loses some of its remembered skills and the patient may lose control of some muscles. Careful exercise can help many stroke victims keep their muscles working.

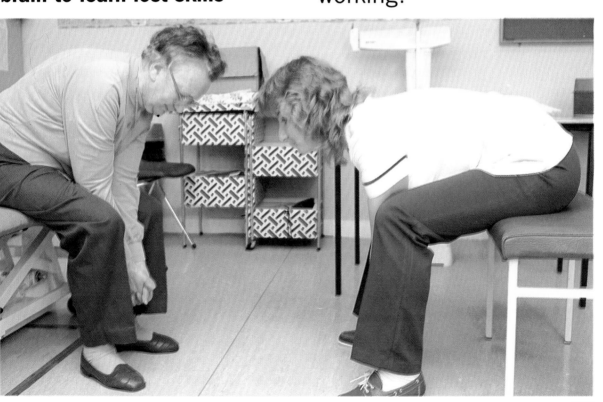

# Treating the Brain

Most illnesses of the brain and nervous system can usually be treated with medicines in a hospital. Samples of blood are taken from the patient and checked in a medical **laboratory** to find out the problem and the correct treatment. If there is a **tumor,** a doctor may decide to operate and cut it out.

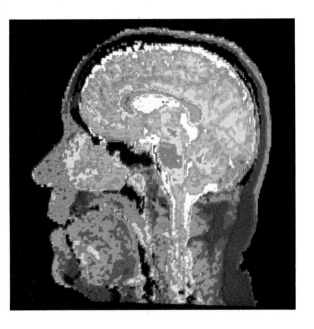

**a scanner's picture of the inside of the brain**

The doctors must know exactly which part of the brain is affected before they can operate. They may decide to take an **X-ray** picture of the brain. They may use a **scanner** to take pictures of slices of brain tissue. The pictures on the screen tell the doctors where to find the damaged parts.

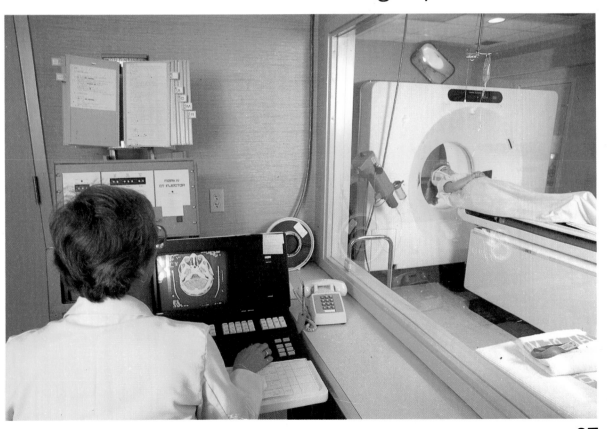

# Understanding the Mind

We know that our minds and our bodies are closely linked together. What affects one affects the other.

Psychologists are people who study how people feel, think, and act. They are interested in how people behave. By discussing their problems with a psychologist or in groups with others, people may be able to see their problems in different ways.

Many problems are caused by the **stress** of modern living, such as traveling to work on the train every day during the rush hour. Psychiatrists study mental illness and its treatment.

**living in high-rise buildings can cause stress which may affect mental health**

# Problems and Care

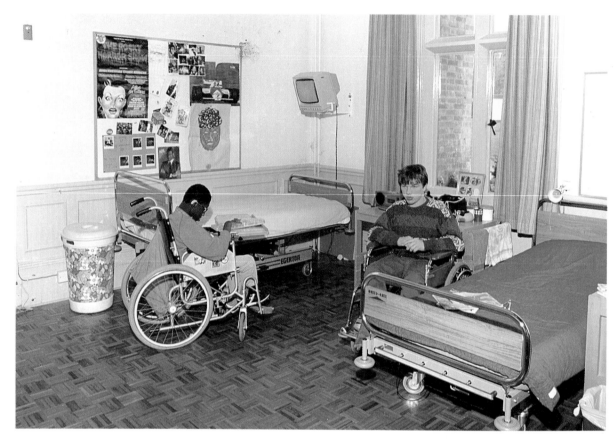

Some people whose brains have been damaged, perhaps at birth, are **mentally handicapped.**

Some live at home with their parents. The handicapped children in this picture live in a special home. They have decorated the wall of their bedroom with posters and photographs.

People with mental handicaps usually have trouble learning, so they are often taught in special schools where they can learn at their own speed.

Today people with mental and physical handicaps are often able to lead rewarding lives.

**handicapped youngsters enjoy a nature trail**

**music often gives pleasure to the mentally handicapped**

# Did You Know?

The heaviest known normal brain belonged to a Russian writer, Ivan Turgenev, who died in 1883. His brain weighed 4.43 pounds.

The smallest known brain belonged to a woman who died in 1977. It weighed 2.42 pounds.

Look at the picture of the tiger and the man and move your eyes toward it until your nose touches the page. The tiger looks

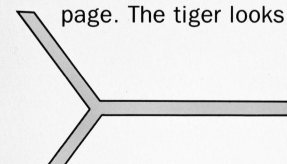

Your brain tries to make sense of what it sees, but it is quite easy to play tricks on it so you think you are seeing something different.
Try some of these tests.

as if it swallows the man! Which is longer, the blue line or the pink? Measure each to see if you are right.

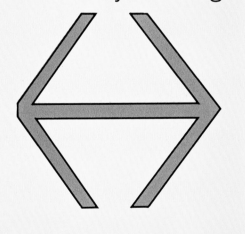

Your brain makes up less than two percent of your body's weight but it uses up 20 percent of the body's energy.

If you look very closely at something you go cross-eyed, because detectors in the eye muscle send signals to the brain.

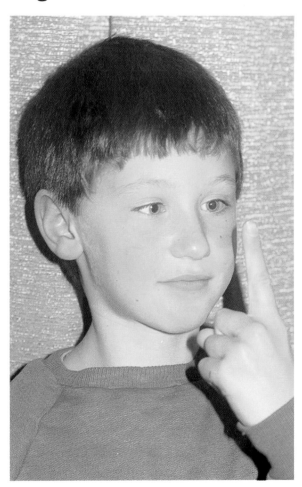

# The Future

A human brain can do more things than any computer yet invented. Computers can only recall the facts they have been given. They cannot think up new ideas or judge whether something is right or wrong. They are controlled by people.

We think that we are the most intelligent creatures on Earth. Beings from a distant planet could be a lot more intelligent than we are. They might not look like us, but they might be intelligent enough to pay us a visit one day!

# Glossary

**adrenal glands**  one of a pair of glands that make hormones to help your body work fast.

**axon**  the long, tail-like part of a nerve cell.

**blood**  a red liquid found inside your body. It carries food, oxygen, and other important things around your body.

**brain**  the "computer" in our heads that controls everything we do.

**brain waves**  the electrical signals from your brain.

**cartilage discs**  rubbery discs between the bones of the spine so they don't rub.

**cell**  a very small part or unit. Most living things are made up of millions of cells.

**central nervous system**  part of the network of nerves in the body. It is made up of the brain and spinal cord.

**cerebellum**  the part of the brain that helps you to stand upright and to move.

**cerebrum**  the part of the brain that controls thinking.

**chemical**  any substance that can change when joined or mixed with another.

**cortex**  the outer layer of the brain made up of the bodies of the nerve cells.

**dendrites**  the branch-like ends of nerve cells.

**digestion**  the breaking down of food for use by the body.

**eardrum**  a tight skin in the ear that is moved by sound.

**electrode**  a substance through which electricity flows.

**endocrine gland**  a group of cells that make hormones.

**epilepsy**  a brain disease that causes someone to fall down, often with violent movements of the body and limbs.

**fiber**  a hair-like or thread-like part of something.

**gray matter**  the more active outer layer of the brain.

**hamstring**  a muscle at the back of the thigh.

**heart**  the part of the body that acts as a pump for the blood.

**hormone**  a substance made in the body to trigger changes such as growth. Hormones are carried in the blood.

**instinct**  knowing how to do things without being taught.

**intelligence**  natural ability to understand and solve things.

**laboratory**  a place used by

46

scientists for experiments.

**medulla**   the part of the body at the bottom of the brain that connects it to the spinal cord.

**membrane**   a thin material that lines or protects body parts.

**meninges**   the membranes that protect the brain and nerves.

**mentally handicapped**   when a person's brain does not work normally.

**microscope**   an instrument that makes very small objects look larger.

**motor**   to do with movement. A motor nerve carries messages from the central nervous system to the muscles.

**muscle**   a type of material that shortens to produce movement.

**nerve**   one of the threads that pass messages between parts of the body and the brain.

**nervous system**   the network of nerves throughout the body.

**neuron**   a nerve cell.

**optic nerve**   the main nerve between the eye and the brain.

**peripheral nervous system**   part of the network of nerves that reaches out to all body parts.

**pituitary gland**   a small part of the body at the base of the brain that makes hormones.

**pons**   a band of nerve fibers that joins the brain together.

**quadriceps**   the big muscle of the front of the thigh.

**reflex**   an action that you do without thinking.

**scanner**   a machine that looks at the insides of something from the outside.

**sense**   one of the natural powers that help a creature to be aware of its surroundings.

**sensory**   to do with the senses. A sensory nerve carries messages from sense organs to the central nervous system.

**spinal cord**   the string of fibers that runs down the inside of the spine.

**stress**   mental pressure.

**stroke**   sudden loss of movement and feeling, usually on one side of the body.

**tumor**   a lump or growth in the body that should not be there.

**virus**   a kind of germ that causes disease when it gets inside the body's cells.

**voluntary**   something that is controlled by thought.

**white matter**   the outer layer of the spinal cord made up of the fibers of the nerve ends.

**X ray**   a light ray that can be used to photograph parts of the body from the outside.

# Index

© Heinemann Children's Reference 1990
Artwork © BLA Publishing Limited 1987

Material used in this book first appeared
in Macmillan World Library: *How Our
Bodies Work: The Brain and Nervous
System.*
Published by Heinemann Children's
Reference.